EMMANUEL JOSEPH

From Pixels to Purpose, How Gaming and Education Can Deepen Spiritual Understanding

Copyright © 2025 by Emmanuel Joseph

All rights reserved. No part of this publication may be reproduced, stored or transmitted in any form or by any means, electronic, mechanical, photocopying, recording, scanning, or otherwise without written permission from the publisher. It is illegal to copy this book, post it to a website, or distribute it by any other means without permission.

First edition

This book was professionally typeset on Reedsy. Find out more at reedsy.com

Contents

1. Chapter 1: The Digital Frontier — 1
2. Chapter 2: The Evolution of Gaming — 3
3. Chapter 3: Learning Through Play — 5
4. Chapter 4: The Role of Narrative — 7
5. Chapter 5: The Power of Immersion — 9
6. Chapter 6: Collaboration and Community — 11
7. Chapter 7: Personal Growth and Development — 13
8. Chapter 8: The Intersection of Gaming and Spirituality — 15
9. Chapter 9: The Role of Reflection and Introspection — 17
10. Chapter 10: The Future of Gaming and Spirituality — 19
11. Chapter 11: Integrating Gaming into Everyday Life — 21
12. Chapter 12: The Journey Ahead — 23
13. Chapter 13: Ethical Considerations in Gaming — 25
14. Chapter 14: The Role of Education in Spiritual Gaming — 27
15. Chapter 15: The Spiritual Journey Continues — 29

1

Chapter 1: The Digital Frontier

In a world where technology is rapidly transforming the way we live, gaming has emerged as a powerful force. From its humble beginnings as a form of entertainment, gaming has evolved into a multifaceted medium that can shape minds and impact lives. It's no longer just about defeating enemies or achieving high scores; it's about immersion in a different reality, learning new skills, and experiencing emotions and stories in unprecedented ways. As we explore this digital frontier, we begin to see the potential it holds for personal growth and spiritual understanding.

Gaming is a unique educational tool that engages players in a way that traditional methods often cannot. The interactive nature of games requires active participation, critical thinking, and problem-solving, which can lead to deeper learning experiences. By immersing players in diverse scenarios and narratives, games can teach empathy, resilience, and strategic thinking. Moreover, they provide a safe space for experimentation and failure, allowing players to learn from their mistakes and grow without real-world consequences.

The spiritual potential of gaming lies in its ability to create meaningful experiences that resonate with players on a deeper level. Games can evoke a sense of wonder, awe, and connection to something greater than oneself. Whether it's through exploring vast, beautifully crafted worlds or engaging with thought-provoking narratives, gaming can inspire introspection and a quest for personal meaning. As players navigate these virtual landscapes, they often confront moral dilemmas and make choices that reflect their values and beliefs, further deepening their spiritual journey.

As we continue to explore the intersection of gaming and education, it becomes clear that these digital experiences have the potential to transform our understanding of spirituality. By harnessing the power of gaming, we can create new opportunities for personal growth and self-discovery, ultimately enriching our spiritual lives.

2

Chapter 2: The Evolution of Gaming

The history of gaming is a testament to human ingenuity and the desire to push the boundaries of what is possible. From the early days of simple arcade games to the complex, immersive experiences of today, gaming has come a long way. This evolution has not only changed the way we play but also the way we learn and perceive the world around us. As technology continues to advance, so too does the potential for gaming to impact our lives in meaningful ways.

In the early days of gaming, the focus was primarily on entertainment and competition. Games like Pong and Space Invaders captured the imagination of players and laid the groundwork for the industry that would follow. As technology improved, so did the complexity and depth of the games being developed. The introduction of home consoles and personal computers revolutionized the way people interacted with games, making them more accessible and varied than ever before.

The rise of online gaming and multiplayer experiences further expanded the potential of the medium. Players could now connect with others from around the world, forging friendships and communities through shared experiences. This social aspect of gaming has been instrumental in fostering a sense of belonging and camaraderie among players. It has also opened up new avenues for collaboration and learning, as players work together to overcome challenges and achieve common goals.

As we look to the future, the possibilities for gaming are virtually limitless. Advances in virtual reality, augmented reality, and artificial intelligence promise to create even more immersive and engaging experiences. These innovations have the potential to transform not only the way we play but also the way we learn and understand the world around us. By embracing the evolution of gaming, we can unlock new opportunities for personal growth and spiritual understanding.

3

Chapter 3: Learning Through Play

The concept of learning through play is not a new one. For centuries, educators have recognized the value of play as a tool for teaching and development. In recent years, gaming has emerged as a powerful extension of this idea, providing a dynamic and engaging platform for learning. By combining the interactive nature of games with educational content, we can create experiences that are both enjoyable and enriching.

One of the key benefits of learning through play is the ability to engage students in a way that traditional methods often cannot. Games can capture the attention and interest of learners, motivating them to explore new concepts and ideas. The interactive nature of games also encourages active participation, critical thinking, and problem-solving, which are essential skills for success in the modern world.

Moreover, games provide a safe space for experimentation and failure, allowing learners to take risks and learn from their mistakes. This is particularly important in the context of spiritual understanding, where personal growth often comes from confronting challenges and reflecting on one's experiences. By creating a supportive and non-judgmental environment, games can help players develop resilience and a deeper sense of self-awareness.

As we continue to explore the potential of gaming as an educational tool, it is important to recognize the unique opportunities it offers for fostering spiritual understanding. By immersing players in meaningful experiences and encouraging introspection, games can inspire a quest for personal meaning and growth. In this way, learning through play can become a powerful catalyst for spiritual development.

4

Chapter 4: The Role of Narrative

Narrative plays a crucial role in the impact of gaming on spiritual understanding. Stories have the power to transport us to different worlds, evoke emotions, and challenge our perspectives. In the context of gaming, narrative can provide a framework for players to explore complex themes and ideas, ultimately leading to a deeper sense of connection and understanding.

In many games, the narrative is woven into the gameplay, creating a seamless and immersive experience. Players become protagonists in their own stories, making choices that shape the outcome and reflect their values and beliefs. This level of agency and involvement can lead to a heightened sense of empathy and self-awareness, as players confront moral dilemmas and consider the consequences of their actions.

The use of narrative in gaming also allows for the exploration of diverse cultures and perspectives. By immersing players in different worlds and experiences, games can foster a greater appreciation for the richness and complexity of the human experience. This can be particularly valuable in the context of spiritual understanding, as it encourages players to consider different viewpoints and question their own beliefs.

As we continue to explore the potential of gaming as a tool for spiritual development, the role of narrative cannot be underestimated. By creating engaging and thought-provoking stories, games can inspire players to reflect on their own lives and experiences, ultimately leading to a deeper sense of purpose and meaning.

5

Chapter 5: The Power of Immersion

Immersion is one of the most powerful aspects of gaming, allowing players to lose themselves in virtual worlds and experiences. This sense of immersion can create a profound connection to the game and its content, making it a valuable tool for spiritual understanding. By fully engaging with the game, players can explore new ideas, confront challenges, and reflect on their own beliefs and values.

One of the key elements of immersion is the ability to create a sense of presence, where players feel as though they are truly part of the game world. This can be achieved through realistic graphics, engaging gameplay, and compelling narratives. The more immersive the experience, the greater the potential for personal growth and spiritual development.

In addition to the technical aspects of immersion, the emotional and psychological impact of gaming cannot be overlooked. Games have the power to evoke a wide range of emotions, from joy and excitement to fear and sadness. By tapping into these emotions, games can create experiences that resonate with players on a deeper level, encouraging introspection and personal growth.

As we continue to explore the potential of gaming as a tool for spiritual understanding, it is important to recognize the unique power of immersion. By creating engaging and immersive experiences, games can inspire players to reflect on their own lives and beliefs, ultimately leading to a deeper sense of purpose and meaning.

6

Chapter 6: Collaboration and Community

The social aspect of gaming is another key factor in its potential for spiritual understanding. Online multiplayer games and gaming communities provide opportunities for players to connect with others, share experiences, and work together towards common goals. This sense of collaboration and community can foster a greater sense of belonging and purpose, ultimately contributing to personal growth and spiritual development.

In many online games, players must work together to overcome challenges and achieve objectives. This requires communication, teamwork, and cooperation, which can help players develop important social skills and a sense of empathy. By collaborating with others, players can learn to appreciate different perspectives and build meaningful relationships, both in and out of the game.

Gaming communities also provide a space for players to share their experiences and learn from one another. Online forums, social media groups, and in-game chat features allow players to discuss strategies, share stories, and offer support. This sense of community can be particularly valuable in the context of spiritual understanding, as it encourages players to reflect on their own beliefs and learn from the experiences of others.

As we continue to explore the potential of gaming as a tool for spiritual development, it is important to recognize the unique opportunities it offers for collaboration and community building. By fostering a sense of connection and belonging, games can inspire players to reflect on their own lives and beliefs, ultimately leading to a deeper sense of purpose and meaning.

7

Chapter 7: Personal Growth and Development

One of the most significant aspects of gaming is its potential to promote personal growth and development. Through engaging gameplay and immersive experiences, players can develop important skills and gain valuable insights into their own lives and beliefs. This process of self-discovery and growth can be particularly valuable in the context of spiritual understanding, as it encourages players to reflect on their own experiences and seek a deeper sense of purpose.

Games often present players with challenges and obstacles that require problem-solving, critical thinking, and resilience. By overcoming these challenges, players can develop a sense of accomplishment and self-efficacy, which can contribute to personal growth and confidence. This process of facing and overcoming difficulties can also help players develop important life skills, such as perseverance and adaptability.

In addition to the cognitive and emotional benefits of gaming, the experiences and stories encountered in games can inspire introspection and personal growth. By immersing players in diverse worlds and narratives, games can encourage them to reflect on their own lives and consider new perspectives. This process of self-reflection can lead to a deeper understanding of one's own beliefs and values, ultimately contributing to spiritual development. Games often present players with challenges and obstacles that require problem-solving, critical thinking, and resilience. By overcoming these challenges, players can develop a sense of accomplishment and self-efficacy, which can contribute to personal growth and confidence. This process of facing and overcoming difficulties can also help players develop important life skills, such as perseverance and adaptability.

In addition to the cognitive and emotional benefits of gaming, the experiences and stories encountered in games can inspire introspection and personal growth. By immersing players in diverse worlds and narratives, games can encourage them to reflect on their own lives and consider new perspectives. This process of self-reflection can lead to a deeper understanding of one's own beliefs and values, ultimately contributing to spiritual development.

Games can also serve as a form of meditation or mindfulness, helping players to focus their attention and cultivate a sense of inner peace. By engaging with games in a mindful way, players can develop a greater awareness of their thoughts and emotions, leading to a deeper sense of self-awareness and spiritual understanding. This mindful approach to gaming can transform the way we interact with digital experiences, turning them into opportunities for personal growth and spiritual exploration.

As we continue to explore the potential of gaming as a tool for personal growth and development, it is important to recognize the unique opportunities it offers for fostering spiritual understanding. By embracing the cognitive, emotional, and reflective aspects of gaming, we can create experiences that inspire players to seek a deeper sense of purpose and meaning in their lives.

8

Chapter 8: The Intersection of Gaming and Spirituality

The intersection of gaming and spirituality is a fascinating and complex area of exploration. As gaming continues to evolve, it offers new opportunities for players to engage with spiritual concepts and deepen their understanding of themselves and the world around them. By incorporating elements of spirituality into games, developers can create experiences that resonate with players on a deeper level, inspiring reflection and personal growth.

Many games already explore spiritual themes and concepts, whether explicitly or implicitly. From games that incorporate mythology and religion into their narratives to those that explore themes of morality, redemption, and self-discovery, there is a rich tapestry of spiritual content in the gaming world. These games provide players with the opportunity to engage with complex ideas and reflect on their own beliefs and values.

The immersive nature of gaming also allows for unique spiritual experiences that can be difficult to achieve through other mediums. By creating virtual worlds that evoke a sense of wonder and awe, games can inspire players to contemplate their place in the universe and their connection to something greater than themselves. This sense of immersion can lead to profound moments of insight and self-discovery, ultimately deepening players' spiritual understanding.

As we continue to explore the intersection of gaming and spirituality, it is important to recognize the potential of games to inspire personal growth and spiritual exploration. By embracing the unique opportunities that gaming offers, we can create experiences that resonate with players on a deeper level and encourage them to seek a deeper sense of purpose and meaning in their lives.

9

Chapter 9: The Role of Reflection and Introspection

Reflection and introspection are essential components of spiritual growth and understanding. By taking the time to reflect on our experiences and consider their deeper meanings, we can gain valuable insights into our own beliefs and values. Gaming provides a unique platform for this process, offering players the opportunity to engage with complex themes and ideas in a meaningful way.

Many games are designed to encourage reflection and introspection, whether through their narratives, gameplay mechanics, or overall design. By presenting players with moral dilemmas, thought-provoking scenarios, and opportunities for self-exploration, games can inspire players to reflect on their own lives and beliefs. This process of introspection can lead to a deeper understanding of oneself and a greater sense of spiritual awareness.

In addition to the reflective aspects of gameplay, the social and collaborative nature of gaming can also contribute to spiritual growth. By engaging with other players and sharing experiences, individuals can gain new perspectives and insights that can help them to better understand their own beliefs and values. This sense of community and shared exploration can be a powerful catalyst for spiritual development.

As we continue to explore the potential of gaming as a tool for reflection and introspection, it is important to recognize the unique opportunities it offers for fostering spiritual understanding. By creating experiences that encourage players to reflect on their own lives and beliefs, we can inspire them to seek a deeper sense of purpose and meaning.

10

Chapter 10: The Future of Gaming and Spirituality

As technology continues to advance, the potential for gaming to impact our spiritual lives is greater than ever. From virtual reality to artificial intelligence, new innovations are creating even more immersive and engaging experiences that can inspire personal growth and spiritual exploration. By embracing these technological advancements, we can unlock new opportunities for players to deepen their understanding of themselves and the world around them.

Virtual reality, in particular, holds great promise for the future of gaming and spirituality. By creating fully immersive environments, VR can transport players to new worlds and experiences, allowing them to explore spiritual concepts in a more profound and meaningful way. This sense of presence and immersion can lead to powerful moments of insight and self-discovery, ultimately deepening players' spiritual understanding.

Artificial intelligence is another area of innovation that has the potential to transform the gaming experience. By creating more dynamic and responsive game worlds, AI can provide players with unique and personalized experiences that cater to their individual needs and interests. This level of personalization can create more meaningful and impactful experiences, fostering personal growth and spiritual exploration.

As we look to the future, it is important to recognize the potential of gaming as a tool for spiritual development. By embracing new technologies and exploring innovative approaches, we can create experiences that inspire players to seek a deeper sense of purpose and meaning in their lives.

11

Chapter 11: Integrating Gaming into Everyday Life

One of the most exciting aspects of gaming is its potential to be integrated into everyday life. As technology becomes more advanced and accessible, gaming can become a seamless part of our daily routines, providing opportunities for personal growth and spiritual exploration. By incorporating gaming into our everyday lives, we can create new ways to engage with spiritual concepts and deepen our understanding of ourselves and the world around us.

Mobile gaming is one example of how gaming can be integrated into everyday life. With the proliferation of smartphones and tablets, players can now access a wide range of games on the go, providing opportunities for learning and reflection throughout the day. By incorporating educational and spiritual content into mobile games, developers can create experiences that inspire personal growth and self-discovery.

Another example of integrating gaming into everyday life is through the use of gamification. By applying game design principles to everyday tasks and activities, we can create more engaging and motivating experiences. This can be particularly valuable in the context of spiritual development, as it encourages individuals to set goals, track their progress, and reflect on their achievements. By making spiritual exploration a more interactive and rewarding experience, gamification can help individuals to develop a deeper sense of purpose and meaning.

As we continue to explore the potential of gaming to be integrated into everyday life, it is important to recognize the unique opportunities it offers for fostering spiritual understanding. By creating experiences that are both engaging and meaningful, we can inspire individuals to seek a deeper sense of purpose and meaning in their lives.

12

Chapter 12: The Journey Ahead

As we conclude our exploration of the potential of gaming and education to deepen spiritual understanding, it is important to recognize that this is just the beginning. The digital frontier is vast and ever-evolving, offering new opportunities for personal growth and spiritual exploration. By embracing the unique potential of gaming, we can create experiences that inspire individuals to seek a deeper sense of purpose and meaning in their lives.

The journey ahead is one of discovery and innovation. As we continue to explore the intersection of gaming, education, and spirituality, we can unlock new opportunities for personal growth and self-discovery. By creating immersive and engaging experiences, we can inspire individuals to reflect on their own lives and beliefs, ultimately leading to a deeper understanding of themselves and the world around them.

As we look to the future, it is important to remain open to new ideas and approaches. The potential of gaming to impact our spiritual lives is vast, and by embracing this potential, we can create experiences that resonate with individuals on a deeper level. By fostering a sense of connection and belonging, we can inspire individuals to seek a deeper sense of purpose and meaning in their lives.

The journey ahead is one of hope and possibility. By embracing the potential of gaming and education to deepen spiritual understanding, we can create a brighter and more meaningful future for ourselves and the world around us.

13

Chapter 13: Ethical Considerations in Gaming

As we explore the potential of gaming to deepen spiritual understanding, it's essential to consider the ethical implications of this rapidly evolving medium. The power of games to influence minds and shape perceptions brings with it a responsibility to ensure that the content is respectful, inclusive, and conducive to personal growth. Ethical considerations in gaming encompass a wide range of issues, from representation and diversity to the impact of violent content and addictive behaviors.

One critical aspect of ethical gaming is the representation of diverse cultures, genders, and identities. Games that include diverse characters and perspectives can foster empathy and understanding among players, contributing to a more inclusive and compassionate gaming community. By creating stories and experiences that reflect the richness and complexity of the human experience, developers can promote a deeper sense of connection and appreciation for diversity.

Another important ethical consideration is the impact of violent content in games. While many games feature combat and conflict as central themes, it's crucial to balance these elements with opportunities for players to reflect on the consequences of their actions. Games that encourage critical thinking and moral decision-making can help players develop a more nuanced understanding of violence and its impact on individuals and communities.

Finally, the potential for gaming addiction and its effects on mental health must be addressed. While gaming can offer valuable opportunities for personal growth and spiritual exploration, it's important to ensure that players maintain a healthy balance between their virtual and real-world lives. Developers and players alike must be mindful of the potential for excessive gaming to interfere with daily responsibilities and overall well-being.

By considering these ethical issues and striving to create responsible and inclusive gaming experiences, we can harness the power of games to foster personal growth and spiritual understanding in a positive and meaningful way.

14

Chapter 14: The Role of Education in Spiritual Gaming

Education plays a crucial role in unlocking the potential of gaming to deepen spiritual understanding. By integrating educational principles and content into games, we can create experiences that not only entertain but also enlighten and inspire. Educational games can serve as powerful tools for teaching spiritual concepts, fostering personal growth, and encouraging reflection and introspection.

One way to incorporate education into spiritual gaming is through the use of serious games, which are designed to teach specific skills or concepts. These games can provide players with valuable insights into various spiritual traditions, philosophies, and practices. By presenting complex ideas in an engaging and interactive format, serious games can make spiritual education more accessible and enjoyable for a wide range of audiences.

Another approach to educational spiritual gaming is through the incorporation of real-world lessons and experiences into gameplay. Games that challenge players to confront moral dilemmas, make difficult choices, and reflect on their actions can help develop critical thinking and ethical reasoning skills. By creating opportunities for players to apply their learning in meaningful ways, educational games can foster a deeper understanding of spiritual concepts and their relevance to everyday life.

In addition to formal educational content, games can also provide informal learning opportunities through exploration and discovery. Open-world games, for example, allow players to immerse themselves in richly detailed environments and uncover hidden stories and secrets. These experiences can inspire curiosity and a sense of wonder, encouraging players to seek out new knowledge and insights.

By integrating educational principles into spiritual gaming, we can create experiences that are both engaging and enlightening, helping players to develop a deeper understanding of themselves and the world around them.

15

Chapter 15: The Spiritual Journey Continues

As we reach the conclusion of our exploration of the potential of gaming and education to deepen spiritual understanding, it is important to recognize that the journey is far from over. The digital frontier offers limitless opportunities for personal growth and spiritual exploration, and the future promises even more exciting possibilities.

The ongoing evolution of technology and game design will continue to shape the landscape of spiritual gaming. As virtual reality, artificial intelligence, and other innovations become more advanced and accessible, we can expect to see increasingly immersive and personalized experiences that cater to individual needs and interests. These advancements will create new opportunities for players to engage with spiritual concepts in profound and meaningful ways.

Moreover, the growing awareness of the potential of gaming as a tool for personal growth and spiritual exploration will inspire more developers to create content that reflects these values. By fostering a sense of purpose and meaning in their games, developers can contribute to a more thoughtful and compassionate gaming community.

As players, educators, and developers, we all have a role to play in shaping the future of spiritual gaming. By embracing the unique potential of gaming to inspire reflection, personal growth, and spiritual understanding, we can create experiences that resonate with individuals on a deeper level and encourage them to seek a greater sense of purpose and meaning in their lives.

The spiritual journey is a lifelong pursuit, and gaming offers a unique and powerful medium for exploring this path. As we continue to navigate the digital frontier, let us remain open to new possibilities and embrace the transformative potential of gaming to deepen our spiritual understanding and enrich our lives.

From Pixels to Purpose: How Gaming and Education Can Deepen Spiritual Understanding

Dive into the digital frontier where pixels merge with purpose and gaming transcends mere entertainment. "From Pixels to Purpose" embarks on a captivating journey through the world of gaming, exploring how this powerful medium, combined with education, can foster profound spiritual growth and understanding. This book delves into the evolution of gaming, the interactive nature of learning through play, and the immersive experiences that can evoke a sense of wonder and connection.

Discover how narrative, collaboration, and community within gaming can inspire empathy, reflection, and personal development. Explore the ethical considerations and the role of education in creating meaningful gaming experiences. As technology continues to advance, the future of gaming holds limitless possibilities for deepening our spiritual lives.

Join us as we navigate this ever-evolving landscape, embracing the unique potential of gaming to inspire a deeper sense of purpose and meaning. Whether you're a gamer, educator, or simply curious about the intersection of technology and spirituality, this book offers valuable insights and practical guidance for integrating gaming into everyday life and embarking on a transformative spiritual journey.

www.ingramcontent.com/pod-product compliance
Lightning Source LLC
LaVergne TN
LVHW010443070526
838199LV00066B/6170